Preface

This book was written because of what God put on my heart: to teach basic skills to help in an emergency situation or a natural disaster. Everything came from all of my experiences that God brought me through to be here with you today.

Not only will this book guide the reader to learn more and encourage them to get outside and discover God's creation, it is my hope that whoever reads this and follows the instructions will come closer to knowing my Lord Jesus.

It is a progressive book that builds on each chapter. Each of the scriptures fits what is being covered in each topic. If, while teaching from this book, you feel led to use more or similar scripture, please do so. The more that we can learn and know God's Word, the better. I want the takeaway for the reader to be this: No matter what you are going through, you are not alone. God can, and will, get you through whatever it is you think that you can't make it through, and will help you be calm and creative through the trying times of your life. As you look back on your life, you will have the perspective to see that God really got you through.

Every time I reflect on my life I remember the poem "Footprints" —of how God carries us even when we can't see Him—and if it wasn't for God, none of what I've learned would be possible. I dedicate this book to three brothers—John, Jerry, and Larry Bridgers—and one grandmother, Ophelia McAlister. Some lessons were harder than others to learn, but knowing God was there with me the whole time is what truly got me through. My grandmother, a woman of strong faith, once told me as we were waiting for a tornado to pass over the house, "If God wants you to come home to heaven; there is nothing that will stop Him." I realized then that God was watching over me all the time. I started taking notice of things in my life as I was growing up. I realized that Philippians 4:13 was truth: "I can do all things through [Christ] who strengthens me." My prayer is you find Him while reading this book and come to know Him as your Savior.

This is a study of the skills needed for you to survive in an emergency situation or natural disaster using outdoor skills and God's Word. You may stretch it out to a chapter a week or read in thirty days. Each chapter will build on the other for the ABC's of

Contents

Preface

1. Direction – Terrain & Maps: Where am I and where am I going?
2. The Rules of 3 in Survival –
3. Shelter – Tent, Tarp, or Debris: Protect myself from the weather
4. Fire – How do I make it if I don't have a lighter?
5. Water – Purified & Filter – I'm thirsty, where do I get a drink?
6. Fishing – Survival Style: The easiest way to get food?
7. Fishing – Rod & Reel: Will I hit the mark?
8. Foiled Again – Using Other Materials to Make Life Easier.
9. Food – Catching, Finding, Cooking, and Utensils: What can I eat?
10. Mental Survival: Am I letting God lead me each day?
11. Signaling for Help: How will they find me?
12. Sleep & Rest – Staying Warm & Dry: Am I re-energizing or not?
13. First Aid – Am I clean?
14. Archery (Protection & Hunting) – How can I provide food?
15. Tools – Do I have tools or do I need to make them?

BONUS CONTENT

Emergency Bag Example   8
Important Knots to Learn   91
Map to Truth   9

Preface

This book was written because of what God put on my heart: to teach basic skills to help in an emergency situation or a natural disaster. Everything came from all of my experiences that God brought me through to be here with you today.

Not only will this book guide the reader to learn more and encourage them to get outside and discover God's creation, it is my hope that whoever reads this and follows the instructions will come closer to knowing my Lord Jesus.

It is a progressive book that builds on each chapter. Each of the scriptures fits what is being covered in each topic. If, while teaching from this book, you feel led to use more or similar scripture, please do so. The more that we can learn and know God's Word, the better. I want the takeaway for the reader to be this: No matter what you are going through, you are not alone. God can, and will, get you through whatever it is you think that you can't make it through, and will help you be calm and creative through the trying times of your life. As you look back on your life, you will have the perspective to see that God really got you through.

Every time I reflect on my life I remember the poem "Footprints" —of how God carries us even when we can't see Him—and if it wasn't for God, none of what I've learned would be possible. I dedicate this book to three brothers—John, Jerry, and Larry Bridgers—and one grandmother, Ophelia McAlister. Some lessons were harder than others to learn, but knowing God was there with me the whole time is what truly got me through. My grandmother, a woman of strong faith, once told me as we were waiting for a tornado to pass over the house, "If God wants you to come home to heaven; there is nothing that will stop Him." I realized then that God was watching over me all the time. I started taking notice of things in my life as I was growing up. I realized that Philippians 4:13 was truth: "I can do all things through [Christ] who strengthens me." My prayer is you find Him while reading this book and come to know Him as your Savior.

This is a study of the skills needed for you to survive in an emergency situation or natural disaster using outdoor skills and God's Word. You may stretch it out to a chapter a week or read in thirty days. Each chapter will build on the other for the ABC's of

Contents

Preface

1. Direction – Terrain & Maps: Where am I and where am I going?   5
2. The Rules of 3 in Survival –   12
3. Shelter - Tent, Tarp, or Debris: Protect myself from the weather   17
4. Fire – How do I make it if I don't have a lighter?   23
5. Water – Purified & Filter – I'm thirsty, where do I get a drink?   32
6. Fishing – Survival Style: The easiest way to get food?   37
7. Fishing – Rod & Reel: Will I hit the mark?   44
8. Foiled Again – Using Other Materials to Make Life Easier.   53
9. Food – Catching, Finding, Cooking, and Utensils: What can I eat?   57
10. Mental Survival: Am I letting God lead me each day?   64
11. Signaling for Help: How will they find me?   67
12. Sleep & Rest – Staying Warm & Dry: Am I re-energizing or not?   72
13. First Aid – Am I clean?   75
14. Archery (Protection & Hunting) – How can I provide food?   82
15. Tools – Do I have tools or do I need to make them?   87

BONUS CONTENT

Emergency Bag Example   88
Important Knots to Learn   91
Map to Truth   92

survival. No matter what happens, no matter what you are going through, if you don't put God first, you won't make it. Whether it be a car wreck, tornado, fire, flood, or hurricane.

Each day is survival. Are we prepared for what may come? James 1:12 says, "Blessed is the one who perseveres under trial because, having stood the test, that person will receive the crown of life that the Lord has promised to those who love him." This is to help you in putting on your "armor" for God (Ephesians 6:10-18). Think of your own testimony and how God has brought you through tough times and how you grew because of it. God doesn't want you to focus on the small thing but to look at the bigger picture.

Teachers, help your students know they can be a leader. This book can also be an adult study—as a guide to bigger and better things. Survival is living through "IT", whatever "IT" is. Life is this world, but living comes through God.

Try to get each child a backpack and first-aid kit. It helps them to know that just like their heart needs filling with God's Word, their pack needs filling with things to survive. Reward them with survival tools when they bring their Bible each week. In the back of the book is a list of survival items that you need. For those who are studying alone, make a bag for yourself.

Things I will need each week of study with my book and backpack:

- **My Bible** - this allows me to be able to look up the scripture and compare it with this book's version.
- **A small note pad and pencil** - to make notes on what God puts on my heart.
- **A heart for God** - this will develop as each week I learn that no matter how bad I think life gets, God is with me.
- **An open mind and ready to listen** - Finding the bigger picture and learning how to wear my armor.

1
Direction – Terrain & Maps
Where am I and where am I going?

Scripture
Proverbs 3:5-6
Trust in the LORD with all your heart and lean not on your own understanding;
in all your ways submit to him, and he will make your
paths straight.

Psalm 119:103-105
How sweet are your words to my taste, sweeter than honey to my mouth!
I gain understanding from your precepts; therefore I hate every wrong path.
Your word is a lamp for my feet, a light on my path.

Jeremiah 6:16
This is what the LORD says:
"Stand at the crossroads and look;
ask for the ancient paths, ask where the good way is, and walk in it, and you will find rest for your souls. But you said, 'We will not walk in it.'"

Luke 15:1-7
Now the tax collectors and sinners were all gathering around to hear Jesus. But the Pharisees and the teachers of the law muttered, "This man welcomes sinners and eats with them." Then Jesus told them this parable: "Suppose one of you has a hundred sheep and loses one of them. Doesn't he leave the ninety-nine in the open country and go after the lost sheep until he finds it? And when he finds it, he joyfully puts it on his shoulders and goes home. Then he calls his friends and neighbors together and says, 'Rejoice with me; I have found my lost sheep.' I tell you that in the same way there will be more rejoicing in heaven over one sinner who repents than over ninety-nine righteous persons who do not need to repent."

Things I need to find my way:

Compass, map, pencil, bright-colored cloth or string and a point to go to.

I may not always have a map but, I will always have God and He will direct my paths.

How do I find basic directions—North, South, East, and West?

There are many ways of doing this, depending on the time of day and where you are located on the planet. Most of the time we are lost and must find our way. If we stop and listen and are still, we can know where we are in life. Listen as you go through this study so that you can find your way.

You need to find North first.

- **Moss grows on the North side of a tree or rock**
    - This depends on where you are located in the hemisphere.
    - Not always the most reliable method.

- **Spider webs**
    - usually on the South side of a tree.
    - also not completely reliable.

- **Shadow Stick**
    - Put a straight stick in the ground and mark where its shadow ends, wait 10 to 15 minutes and mark where the shadow is then. The two points should give you East & West, then you can find North.

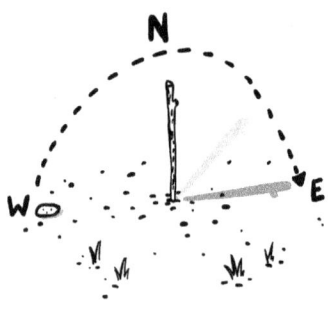

Where is the Sun?

- If it is morning, the Sun comes up in the East and it sets in the West.
- Different times of the year the Sun travels at different points in the sky, due to seasons and where you are on the planet.

Make a rough compass

- If you have a pan of water (pool of water), a needle, stick pin, or paper clip, and a small leaf.

- Rub the pin (metal) really fast for about 30 seconds on your jeans or a fleece-like jacket (this helps magnetize it)

- Set the pin on the leaf and put it in the pan of water or a puddle of calm water. It will point North and South.

Use your compass!

- It doesn't have to be a fancy compass; you are just trying to find which way you are going.

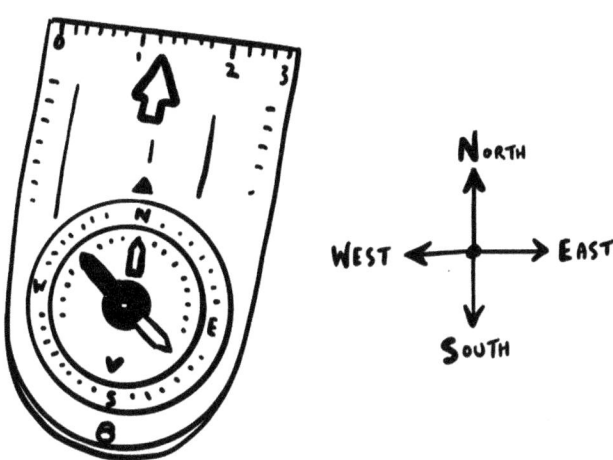

This is just like God's Word. You have to open it in order to find your direction (Proverbs 3:5-6).

How has God led you in your direction in life?
Are you traveling in the right direction that God wants you to go?

_____
_____
_____

How do you know what direction He is leading you in?

"Be still and know that I am God . . ." (Psalm 46:10).

He is our guide, our strength, and our fortress.

Read His Word each day and you will see your path.

A Topography Map gives you land marks and distance by the lines on the map. Always get a local paper map of the area you are going to be in. You may not have cell service to use a map app.

Always look for the legend so you can read the map.
- Roads
- Water
- Elevation
- Locations
- Cities or towns
- Landmarks
- Buildings and city boundaries.

A Street Map gives streets, towns, miles, and landmarks. Again, always look for the legend so that you can read the map.

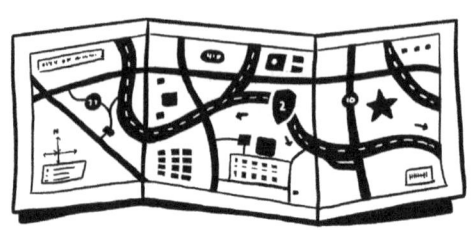

- Roads
- Cities or Communities
- Places
- Parks
- Water

Figure out where you are and then head to a place that you can find help or a phone.

Be sure to stay hydrated whenever you take off on your trek. Keep a bearing from where you started and where you are going. It is easy to get off of the path. It is better to travel in straight lines to make sure you don't get off track. Even if you are off by 2 degrees, you can end up a mile off track.

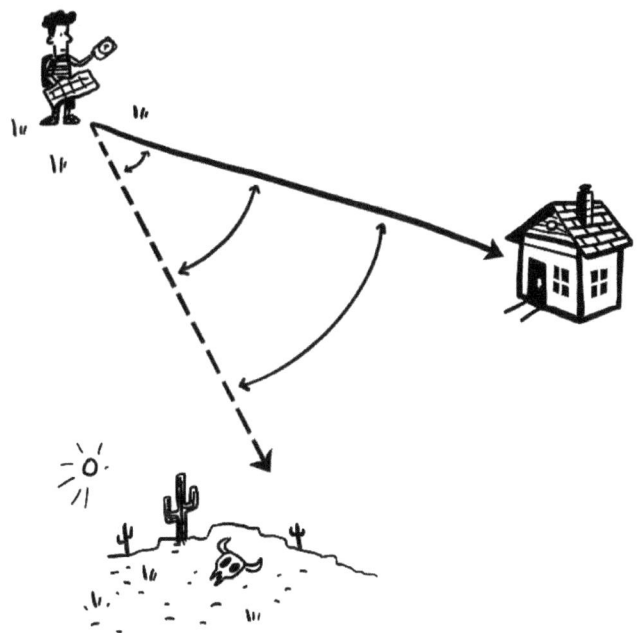

Example: after I have only gone about 10 yards, I'm already off track by a couple of feet. Use markers, string, a torn rag, but mark your trail—you don't want to get lost trying to find help. This also helps others find you if you leave markers for your trail.

Let God be your guide in your life: John 16:13.
Have you found your path? Where is God sending you?

2
The Rules of 3 in Survival

Am I thinking ahead? What is in my bag? What are my resources?

God's holy number is the number 3. He created us by that number
—Father, Son, and Holy Spirit.
He will always lead you if you just follow.

Scripture
Ephesians 6:10-11
Finally, be strong in the Lord and in his mighty power. Put on the full armor of God, so that you can take your stand against the devil's schemes.

Ephesians 6:14-18
Stand firm then, with the belt of truth buckled around your waist, with the breastplate of righteousness in place, and with your feet fitted with the readiness that comes from the gospel of peace. In addition to all this, take up the shield of faith, with which you can extinguish all the flaming arrows of the evil one. Take the helmet of salvation and the sword of the Spirit, which is the word of God. And pray in the Spirit on all occasions with all kinds of prayers and requests. With this in mind, be alert and always keep on praying for all the Lord's people.

Psalm 23:1-5
The LORD is my shepherd, I lack nothing.
He makes me lie down in green pastures, he leads me beside quiet waters, He refreshes my soul. He guides me along the right paths for his name's sake. Even though I walk through the darkest valley, I will fear no evil, for you are with me; your rod and your staff, they comfort me. You prepare a table before me in the presence of my enemies. You anoint my head with oil; my cup overflows.

Matthew 4:4
Jesus answered, "It is written: 'Man shall not live on bread alone, but on every word that comes from the mouth of God.'"

The Rules of 3 of Survival to Stay Alive:
3 minutes – without air or in icy water
3 hours – without shelter from the weather
3 days – without water (clean water)
3 weeks – without food (but you have water)

All of these things bring death. Follow God's rules to stay alive.

Can you think of a time where God was watching over you?
_____
_____
_____

Things to Know:
- The average person needs to drink proper amounts of water a day, and when you eat food, you use your water for digestion.
- A person needs shelter to protect themselves from wind, rain, and critters.
- Laying on the ground without an air barrier will drain the heat out of your body and you will get hypothermia and die.
- You must consume about 1,000 to 1,200 calories of food a day. If you are on the move, walking, building a shelter, or working (exerting yourself), you need about 2,000 to 3,000 calories a day to survive.
- Each person is different. Some of us have allergies, so certain foods wouldn't work. You need to always consume some kind of protein every day. Protein builds muscle and helps you regenerate.

Items that can sustain you over a short period of time:

FOOD
- Protein bars
- Peanut butter crackers
- Tuna packets (do NOT leave these in the heat, they will go bad)
- Cans of soup
- Green leafy plants (edibles that have been tested)
- Freeze-dried foods

- Beef, chicken, or turkey jerky
- Dried beans (soak in water for 12 hours and then cook until tender to eat)
- Rice

WATER
- Always make sure your water is filtered and purified by boiling.

CLOTHES
- Stay warm and dry. If you get wet, you need to dry your clothes.
- Always carry a change of clothes and 2 pairs of socks.
- You need a small blanket.
- You need a rain poncho. This can keep you dry in the rain, and it can become a tent or a tarp for a shelter.

TOOLS
- Compass
- Some sort of cutting tool (cutting, sawing, hammering, poking, grabbing tools)
- Fire-starting supplies
- Water bottle
- First aid kit
- A metal container

Genesis 41:49 - Prepare for what comes, and God will get you through with whatever you brought, but, you must . . .

BE PREPARED!

It's kind of like becoming a Christian.
You have to prepare your heart, mind, and soul.
What are you bringing to do that?
Do you feel guilty that you have sinned?
Are you reading God's Word? Are you fellowshipping with other Christians?

Do you know the ABC's to becoming a Christian?

A - **Admit** I'm a sinner - I need God in control of my life

B - **Believe** that Jesus is the Son of God, died for my sins, and rose again to be my Lord and Savior!

C - **Confess** publicly that I am a Christian and follow Jesus

Well, survival is very similar to your walk with Christ. Just like the ABC's of Christianity, there are the **ABC's of survival**.

A - Admit I'm not alone - Emmanuel - God is with us

B - Believe that God will get me through this

C - Be calm and be creative because God is in control

Trusting in God will get you through anything. Just like the hope that Christ brought when He was born, God brings hope that He will get you through whatever the world throws at you. But it takes action on your part. We must come to Him in order for Him to help us.

Who is Jesus to you? How do you know Jesus? What does He ask of you?

_____
_____
_____
_____
_____
_____
_____

Survival is getting through the tough times in life—it is the short term. But where are you going to be for the rest of your life—the long term? Am I going to be that person that only calls on God in those short-term times in my life or do I want Him in control of my whole life?

What are your thoughts?

_____
_____
_____
_____
_____
_____
_____

3
Shelter: Tent, Tarp, or Debris
How do I protect myself from the weather?

It is vital that you are able to stay out of the weather and the wind, and you have a place to sleep and rest
(just like Psalm 23:2 says).

How will you make it and survive, if you're not resting and staying warm?

Scripture
Psalm 91:1-6
Whoever dwells in the shelter of the Most High will rest in the shadow of the Almighty.
I will say of the LORD, "He is my refuge and my fortress, my God, in whom I trust."
Surely he will save you from the fowler's snare and from the deadly pestilence.
He will cover you with his feathers, and under his wings you will find refuge; his faithfulness will be your shield and rampart.
You will not fear the terror of night, nor the arrow that flies by day,
nor the pestilence that stalks in the darkness, nor the plague that destroys at midday.

Exodus 9:18-19
"Therefore, at this time tomorrow I will send the worst hailstorm that has ever fallen on Egypt, from the day it was founded till now. Give an order now to bring your livestock and everything you have in the field to a place of shelter, because the hail will fall on every person and animal that has not been brought in and is still out in the field, and they will die."

Genesis 33:16-18
So that day Esau started on his way back to Seir. Jacob, however, went to Sukkoth, where he built a place for himself and made shelters for his livestock. That is why the place is called Sukkoth.

After Jacob came from Paddan Aram, he arrived safely at the city of Shechem in Canaan and camped within sight of the city.

Psalm 18:30-31
As for God, his way is perfect: The LORD's word is flawless; he shields all who take refuge in him. For who is God besides the LORD? And who is the Rock except our God?

What kinds of shelters are possible?

A shelter depends on your supplies. What do I have to make a shelter with? Do I have the tools? Do I need tools? How long will I be in this location? How much daylight do I have? All of these things play a factor in your shelter building. You want to be at least 200 feet from your water source, and remember . . . use the bathroom at least a 100 to 200 feet from your shelter area. And NEVER use the bathroom near your water source!!!

You need:
- Cordage (string, vines, twine, cord, or rope)
- Strong branches, and trees close together.

Study the pictures of different shelters that you can create. It just depends on your time and materials.

REMEMBER, you are trying to keep the wind, rain, and critters from getting to you in the night.

Where am I?
and...
What are my options?

- Tent
- Tarp
- Poncho
- Lean-to
- Teepee or Wigwam
- Debris shelter

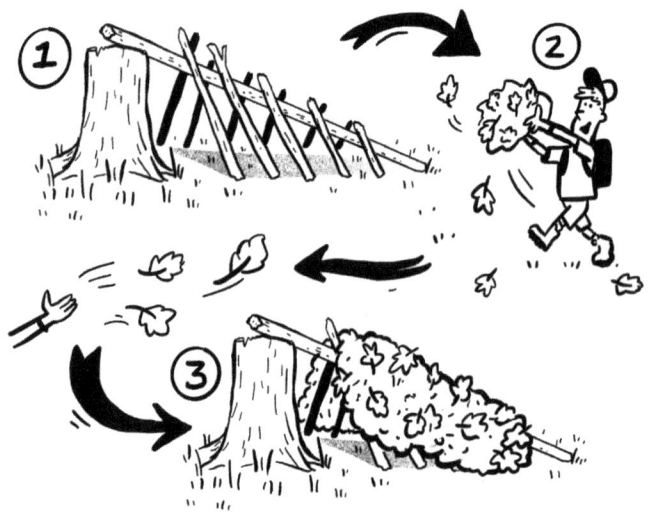

Do I have to have tools to build a shelter?

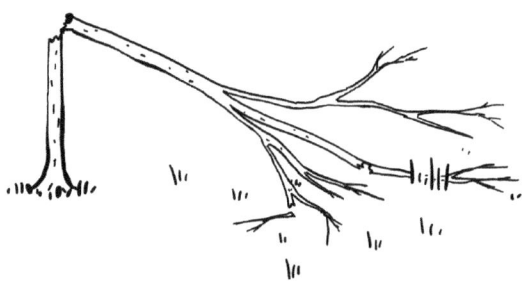

NO, but it does help.

You can break limbs with other trees. Find trees that are down, and you already have what you need. Use the resources around you. You can use vines, tall green grass, and some tree barks for your cordage (rope).

Remember, there are always resources.

God is the Great Provider. There are resources all around you. Native Americans didn't have chainsaws, tents, refrigerators, cell phones, etc.

Remember it is the Big Picture that God wants you to see and feel in your heart. He is the Great Creator—look around at all that He gives you.

What has God given me for a bed, roof, walls, and to make my fire with?
Where are your resources? What are my surroundings? Which way is the wind blowing?

Are you using all that God has given you?

_____

_____

_____

_____

_____

Are you opening your heart to Him? Are you paying attention and listening to Him?

Ask yourself, What has God given me?

_____

_____

_____

_____

_____

_____

4

Fire

How do I make fire it if I don't have a lighter?
(You have to be tinder with it)

WARNING:

FIRE IS VERY DANGEROUS.

IT CAN CAUSE INJURY OR DEATH.
FIRE CAN ALSO CAUSE DAMAGE TO PROPERTY AND LAND.

NEVER PLAY WITH FIRE.

ALWAYS HAVE ADULT SUPERVISION.

Fire is important for many reasons. It keeps us warm when it is cold. It allows us to boil water and cook food. It keeps critters away. It also creates charcoal to strain and purify water. We can use it to signal for help. Fire is important.

Scripture
Genesis 22:5-9
He said to his servants, "Stay here with the donkey while I and the boy go over there. We will worship and then we will come back to you." Abraham took the wood for the burnt offering and placed it on his son Isaac, and he himself carried the fire and the knife. As the two of them went on together, Isaac spoke up and said to his father Abraham, "Father?" "Yes, my son?" Abraham replied. "The fire and wood are here," Isaac said, "but where is the lamb for the burnt offering?" Abraham answered, "God himself will provide the lamb for the burnt offering, my son." And the two of them went on together. When they reached the place God had told him about, Abraham built an altar there and arranged the wood on it. He bound his son Isaac and laid him on the altar, on top of the wood.

Deuteronomy 1:32-33
In spite of this, you did not trust in the LORD your God, who went ahead of you on your journey, in fire by night and in a cloud by day, to search out places for you to camp and to show you the way you should go.

Job 28:4-5
Far from human dwellings they cut a shaft, in places untouched by human feet; far from other people they dangle and sway. The earth, from which food comes, is transformed below as by fire.

Acts 28:2-4
The islanders showed us unusual kindness. They built a fire and welcomed us all because it was raining and cold. Paul gathered a pile of brushwood and, as he put it on the fire, a viper, driven out by the heat, fastened itself on his hand. When the islanders saw the snake hanging from his hand, they said to each other, "This man must be a murderer; for though he escaped from the sea, the goddess Justice has not allowed him to live."

- WARNING -
FIRE is VERY DANGEROUS!

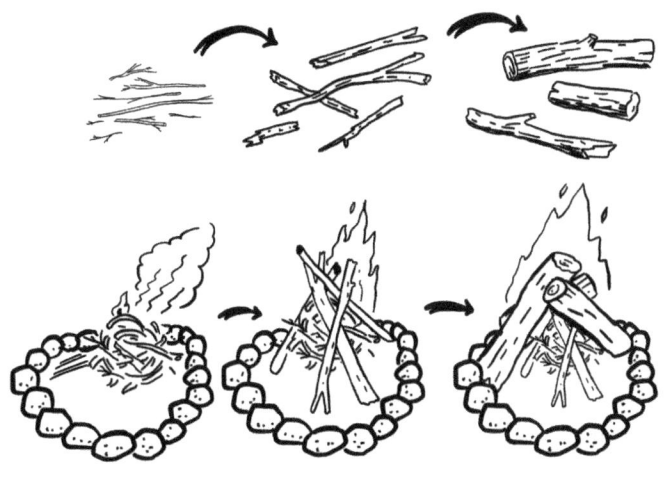

ALWAYS HAVE ADULT SUPERVISION and NEVER play with Fire.

So what do I need to get a fire started?

Tinder, twigs, small sticks, big sticks, and firewood. You can make tinder from a bird nest, grass, hand sanitizer, cotton balls, potato chips, shavings from cedar bark or cotton wood trees, cloth fibers, shavings from a stick with a pencil sharpener or knife, paper, or leaves.

The tinder bundle MUST BE DRY. You want to make sure it can get air to it as you catch it on fire. Twigs are the next thing you want to get—small twigs, like matchstick size. These also need to be dry. You want to have at least 3 handfuls of twigs, like 3 little bundles of wood. You can gather this material while getting wood for your shelter.

Put your tinder bundle at the bottom. You may need to make a stick or bark platform to put it on, depending on how wet the ground is at the time. Now you need some small sticks.

Always try to put a barrier of rocks or logs around your fire area. It is best if you can dig a small hole to build your fire in. It will depend on the terrain you are on whether that is possible.

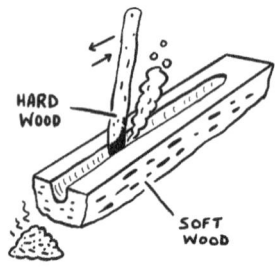

What does make fire?

A flammable and

Push the rod back and forth very fast to cause friction and make an ember.

Scrape a small pile of magnesium into your tender bundle, now strike the rod on the back of the magnesium block.

it take to

item, oxygen, wood to

burn. That is the basics of a fire.

There are many ways to setup your fire, because you want to make sure it gets air, here are some examples:

There are different ways to start a fire, once you have your fire materials and a safe location.

The Fire Plow

Flint & Magnesium

Ferro Rod

Make a tinder bundle shape like a bird's nest. Use either the piece of metal or the back of your knife (the non-sharp end). Strike the rod to make sparks.

FIRE is NOTHING to PLAY with, it is for SURVIVAL.

Waterproof Matches
Waterproof matches must be dry to work.

Magnifying Glass
The magnifying glass must have good sunlight to be effective.

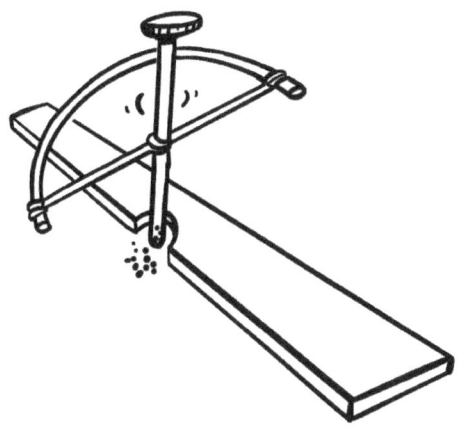

Bow Drill
(this is advanced)

The bow drill has many parts, a soft wood for the bottom board, a hardwood rod with 2 sharpened ends, a hand cap, and a bow. It creates friction to make an ember in the notched soft wood board.

AA Battery and gum wrapper
You can cut the wrapper in an hour-glass shape

A 9-volt battery and steel wool
Create a short and a spark for a flammable material to burn.

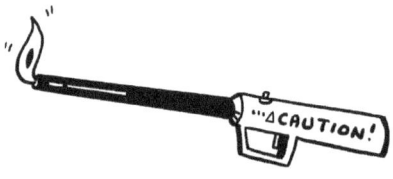

And of course the easiest way is with a lighter.

Fire keeps me warm, gives me light, keeps animals away, cooks my food, and boils my water to make it pure.

Another great thing you can build for your fire and shelter area is a fire wall. This will keep the smoke from constantly blowing on you, and it will keep it warmer at your shelter.

This can be done with a stack of logs or with stone. It creates a place for the air to rise instead of being blown around by the wind. This is the ideal setup for your shelter area.

Fire is your warmth and your light. Just like Jesus can be the light in you. People can see your fire from a distance. Can people see the light of Jesus in you? Is it a flicker or a roaring fire?

Fire takes fuel, just like the fire inside you needs fuel. How are you fueling your fire for Jesus?

What do you need to do to make your fire be seen by others?

_____
_____
_____

5
Water: Purified & Filtered
I'm thirsty, where do I get a drink?

So many times we see something and think everything is okay but, in truth it is not what it seems. Just because water looks clean doesn't mean it is drinkable. Just like us, we have to be purified. Knowing what to do is half the battle, do what is Right, not what is Easy.

Scripture
John 4:13-15
Jesus answered, "Everyone who drinks this water will be thirsty again, but whoever drinks the water I give them will never thirst. Indeed, the water I give them will become in them a spring of water welling up to eternal life." The woman said to him, "Sir, give me this water so that I won't get thirsty and have to keep coming here to draw water."

Acts 2:38-39
Peter replied, "Repent and be baptized, every one of you, in the name of Jesus Christ for the forgiveness of your sins. And you will receive the gift of the Holy Spirit. The promise is for you and your children and for all who are far off—for all whom the Lord our God will call."

Psalm 119:65-67
Do good to your servant according to your word, Lord.
Teach me knowledge and good judgment, for I trust your commands.
Before I was afflicted I went astray, but now I obey your word.

Isaiah 30:14-15
"It will break in pieces like pottery, shattered so mercilessly that among its pieces not a fragment will be found for taking coals from a hearth or scooping water out of a cistern." This is what the Sovereign Lord, the Holy One of Israel, says: "In repentance and

rest is your salvation, in quietness and trust is your strength, but you would have none of it.

Luke 8:4-15
While a large crowd was gathering and people were coming to Jesus from town after town, he told this parable: "A farmer went out to sow his seed. As he was scattering the seed, some fell along the path; it was trampled on, and the birds ate it up. Some fell on rocky ground, and when it came up, the plants withered because they had no moisture. Other seed fell among thorns, which grew up with it and choked the plants. Still other seed fell on good soil. It came up and yielded a crop, a hundred times more than was sown." When he said this, he called out, "Whoever has ears to hear, let them hear." His disciples asked him what this parable meant. He said, "The knowledge of the secrets of the kingdom of God has been given to you, but to others I speak in parables, so that, 'though seeing, they may not see; though hearing, they may not understand.' This is the meaning of the parable: The seed is the word of God. Those along the path are the ones who hear, and then the devil comes and takes away the word from their hearts, so that they may not believe and be saved. Those on the rocky ground are the ones who receive the word with joy when they hear it, but they have no root. They believe for a while, but in the time of testing they fall away. The seed that fell among thorns stands for those who hear, but as they go on their way they are choked by life's worries, riches and pleasures, and they do not mature. But the seed on good soil stands for those with a noble and good heart, who hear the word, retain it, and by persevering produce a crop.

Is water important to us for living?

We consist of about 70% water; the planet is covered by 78% water. So yes, we need enough water each day to stay properly hydrated.

Where can I get water to drink if I run out?

There are many ways to obtain water in an **emergency situation.**
- Well
- Creek or River
- Pond or Lake
- Spring or Rock Face
- Condensation
- Rain Catchment

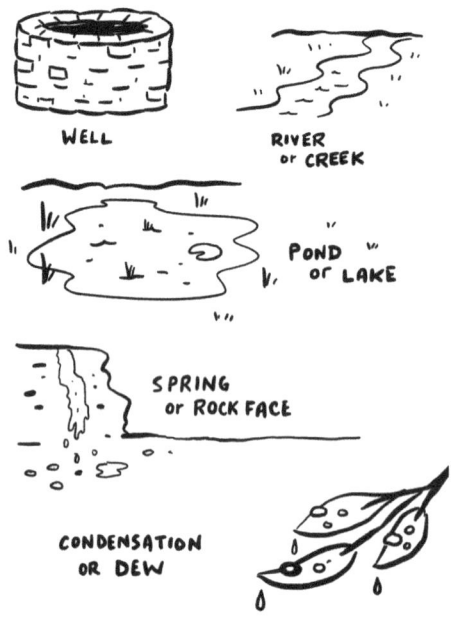

CAUTION! NEVER TRUST that the water is PURE. It is important to filter and then purify the water.

There are some methods that will do both at the same time, like a water filter or a filter straw, but you may not have that as a resource. Here are some ways to make sure the water is pure and filtered.

- Filter or Filter Straw
- Homemade Filter
- Tree Branch Filter
- Wicking Filter
- Sip Well Creekside
- Chemical - Iodine/Chlorine
- Boil water
- Solar Purify

Vegetation can filter water. But it is important to remember water from a creek may LOOK clean, but you don't know what fell in the water from upstream or what is behind the rocks. Never get your water near an area where animals have been drinking because, they will use the bathroom in the water.

It is best, if you don't have a store-bought filter, to filter it with some kind of cloth or homemade filter and then boil your water, just to make sure, you don't get any disease or germs.

You can build your own filter by taking a two-liter bottle and cutting the bottom out of it. Put a cloth in the top of the bottle, then take charcoal from your fire (crushed up as fine as possible) and put a couple handfuls full in your bottle, now put a couple handfuls of sand, add a couple handfuls of small gravel, then put in some large rocks and add some moss or grass to filter your water. Poke a couple of holes in the bottle top and tie cordage to the bottom of the bottle where you cut off the bottle filter so you can hang it from a tree limb. Now get some water and pour it in. You should have time to put the bottle you just used underneath the filter to capture your clean water. You may have to run it through twice. You have now made a water filter.

Each piece has purpose. Just like you have a purpose.
If you don't drink clean water, you will get sick and die of dehydration.

We are like the water. We need to be cleaned from our sins. That is why Jesus died for us.

He shed His blood, cleansed (filtered) our sins out, and purified us. Do you know Him? God can't be around sin. Do you have sin that is keeping you from Him?

_____
_____
_____

6
Fishing – Survival Style
What is going to be the easiest way to get food?

Fishing is probably the easiest method of catching and getting protein, other than eating bugs and worms or grubs. Protein is very important to help keep your strength in a survival situation. Freshwater fish can have parasites in them so, they must be cooked. Salt water fish don't, but to be safe it is best to cook all.

Scripture
Job 38:34-41
"Can you raise your voice to the clouds and cover yourself with a flood of water? Do you send the lightning bolts on their way? Do they report to you, 'Here we are'? Who gives the ibis wisdom or gives the rooster understanding? Who has the wisdom to count the clouds? Who can tip over the water jars of the heavens when the dust becomes hard and the clods of earth stick together? "Do you hunt the prey for the lioness and satisfy the hunger of the lions when they crouch in their dens or lie in wait in a thicket? Who provides food for the raven when its young cry out to God and wander about for lack of food?"

1 Peter 4:10-13
Each of you should use whatever gift you have received to serve others, as faithful stewards of God's grace in its various forms. If

anyone speaks, they should do so as one who speaks the very words of God. If anyone serves, they should do so with the strength God provides, so that in all things God may be praised through Jesus Christ. To him be the glory and the power for ever and ever. Amen. Dear friends, do not be surprised at the fiery ordeal that has come on you to test you, as though something strange were happening to you. But rejoice inasmuch as you participate in the sufferings of Christ, so that you may be overjoyed when his glory is revealed.

Jeremiah 16:15-17
"But it will be said, 'As surely as the LORD lives, who brought the Israelites up out of the land of the north and out of all the countries where he had banished them.' For I will restore them to the land I gave their ancestors.
"But now I will send for many fishermen," declares the LORD, "and they will catch them. After that I will send for many hunters, and they will hunt them down on every mountain and hill and from the crevices of the rocks. My eyes are on all their ways; they are not hidden from me, nor is their sin concealed from my eyes."

Matthew 7:9-11
"Which of you, if your son asks for bread, will give him a stone? Or if he asks for a fish, will give him a snake? If you, then, though you are evil, know how to give good gifts to your children, how much more will your Father in heaven give good gifts to those who ask him!"

It will not be easy but, you must trust that God will provide.

So what do you need to catch a fish?

Different fish are caught different ways. We are going to go through some different ways of catching fish without a rod and reel—using fishing lines, nets, snares, and baskets.

What are my resources?

Dental floss, an aluminum can, a mesh laundry bag, and my survival knife or cutting tool. These materials will give you 5 different ways of catching fish.

Homemade Fishing Pole

1. Take your cutting tool and cut down a small tree that is about as big around as the top of a soft drink bottle top. It needs to be about 1 foot taller than you but, not more than 6 feet long. You can also use bamboo, if available.

2. Now take your dental floss or cordage and cut off 2 to 3 times the length of your new pole. Make a notch about 2 or 3 inches from the end of the pole, all the way around the pole. This will give you a groove to put your dental floss or cordage in and tie it with a fisherman's knot.

3. Now we need a cork. To make your cork, look around the water and you should find driftwood, it is usually gray. It is

really light and will float. Tie the same knot around it about 2 feet from the end of your line on the pole. This will become your cork.

4. Now we need a hook. You can use a safety pin if you have one, but most of the time we can't find one, so we are going to make a hook from the soda can tab on the top of the can. Break off the tab and bend the end with the opening you use to pry up the tab when you drink a soda. It is easier if you take your cutting tool and try and cut where you want to bend it and then it will bend easier. Also, you want to tie this knot on to your new hook (fisherman knot). (see knot guide in chapter

Homemade Fishing Net

1. Take your cutting tool and cut a tree limb that has a "Y" shape at the end about as tall as you. Kind of like a switch but you want the big end to be about the size of a soda bottle top.

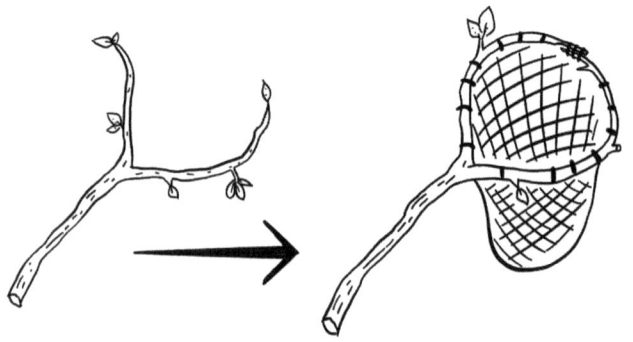

2. Take the two ends of the switch and take the leaves off. Bend the two ends together to make a loop. Tie the looped

ends together with your cordage so that you have something to tie your laundry bag to.

3. Once you have your loop take your dental floss or the string in the laundry bag and tie around where you made your loop. Make sure it is really tight. You may have to tie it in a couple of places to keep it strong—remember it has to hold the weight of your fish.

Homemade Fishing Spear

1. This is a little harder and you have to be really good at throwing a spear, but you can do it. Cut a straight limb or small tree that is a little bigger than a soda bottle top. You will also need 2 smaller sticks as wide as the palm of your hand and as big around as your index finger. You will also need your cutting tool and cordage.

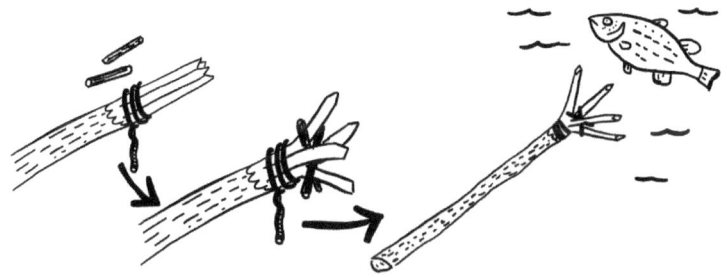

2. Carefully take one end of the stick and split it into fourths about 3 or 4 inches, the length of your index finger doubled—this will give you 4 ends on the stick. Now wrap some cordage around the stick where the split ends.

3. Now take one of your small sticks and push it down through where you split the stick in half, then take the

other small stick and push it through the other half, so it forms a cross. Then you need to take your cordage and tie them into place. Using your cutting tool, sharpen all 4 points of the spear.

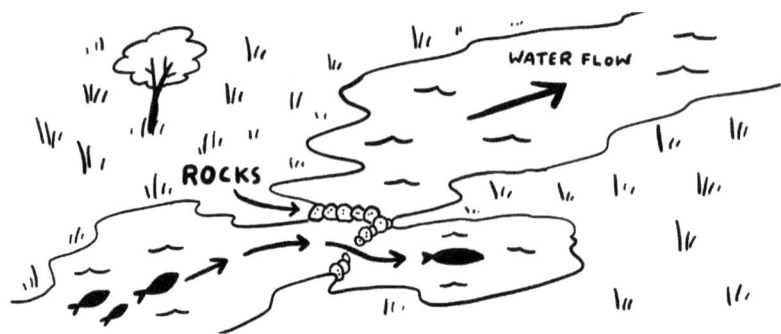

4. Be sure NOT to cut yourself. Sharpen the points on the outside and inside of the points of the spear. What this

does is gives you more points while stabbing your fish. You can burn the tips when you are finished to harden the spear ends, but be careful not to do it too much and burn your cordage.

Fishing Trap

1. This is good to do when there is a creek or stream where fish are swimming. You block off the water where if forces the water to go through your trap and make it so the fish can't swim out of the trap.

2. Make your barrier out of sticks or your net or even rocks. This will catch fish while you are building your shelter or making fire or gathering other food, like plants, to eat.

How do I cook what I caught?

Once you catch your fish, make sure it is dead. It is really hard to clean the fish to eat when it is still alive. Be sure to cut the head off behind the gills. Then cut down the middle of the belly area and remove the insides. You can cook it with the scales still on it, you just have to be careful and not eat that part. It doesn't taste good and is not healthy to eat.

WATCH FOR BONES! Remember there is no one there to help you if you choke on a bone.

Jesus made the disciples fishers of men. Where are you in the service of Christ? Are you just trying to feed yourself or are you letting others see Him in you? Christ promises that He will provide what you need the very hour you need it (Luke 12:11-12).

7

Fishing Rod & Reel
Will I hit the mark or be tangled in the weeds?

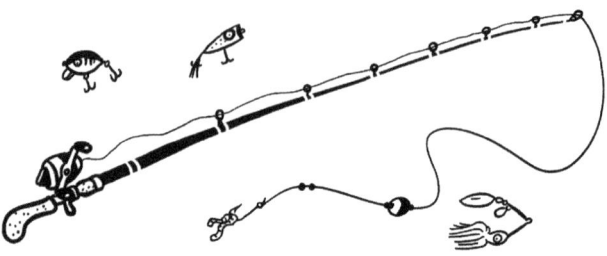

Scripture
Control
2 Chronicles 17:3-6
The LORD was with Jehoshaphat because he followed the ways of his father David before him. He did not consult the Baals but sought the God of his father and followed his commands rather than the practices of Israel. The LORD established the kingdom under his control; and all Judah brought gifts to Jehoshaphat, so that he had great wealth and honor. His heart was devoted to the ways of the LORD; furthermore, he removed the high places and the Asherah poles from Judah.

Patience
Romans 2:3-5
So when you, a mere human being, pass judgment on them and yet do the same things, do you think you will escape God's judgment? Or do you show contempt for the riches of his
kindness, forbearance and patience, not realizing that God's kindness is intended to lead you to repentance? But because of your stubbornness and your unrepentant heart, you are storing up wrath against yourself for the day of God's wrath, when his righteous judgment will be revealed.

Timing
Ecclesiastes 3:1-13

There is a time for everything, and a season for every activity under the heavens:

2   a time to be born and a time to die, a time to plant and a time to uproot,
3   a time to kill and a time to heal, a time to tear down and a time to build,
4   a time to weep and a time to laugh, a time to mourn and a time to dance,
5   a time to scatter stones and a time to gather them, a time to embrace and a time to refrain from embracing,
6   a time to search and a time to give up, a time to keep and a time to throw away,
7   a time to tear and a time to mend, a time to be silent and a time to speak,
8   a time to love and a time to hate, a time for war and a time for peace.
9 What do workers gain from their toil? 10 I have seen the burden God has laid on the human race. 11 He has made everything beautiful in its time. He has also set eternity in the human heart; yet no one can fathom what God has done from beginning to end.

Practice & Perseverance
Hebrews 10:19-25

Therefore, brothers and sisters, since we have confidence to enter the Most Holy Place by the blood of Jesus, by a new and living way opened for us through the curtain, that is, his body, and since we have a great priest over the house of God, let us draw near to God with a sincere heart and with the full assurance that faith brings, having our hearts sprinkled to cleanse us from a guilty conscience and having our bodies washed with pure water. Let us hold unswervingly to the hope we profess, for he who promised is faithful. And let us consider how we may spur one another on toward love and good deeds, not giving up meeting together, as some are in the habit of doing, but encouraging one another—and all the more as you see the Day approaching.

Three Different Kinds of Rod & Reel

Spinning Reel   Bait Cast Reel   Spin-cast Reel

Each kind of reel has a right way to use it. Some are designed for faster casts, some for casting farther, and some for pull or drag while fishing. Most of the time your reel is already mounted to a good rod when you buy it from the store. If you are fortunate to have this gear in a survival situation, it is very good.

Lessons of life to apply:
"Faster is not always better. There are no shortcuts to life. We can make things easier, but there are no shortcuts."

Having a rod and reel does not mean that you will automatically catch fish. Fishing takes Control, Patience, Timing, and Practice, whether you are using a net or a rod & reel. Just like learning God's Word.

Can you list times where you needed to have Control, Patience, Timing, and Practice?

_____
_____
_____

Spinning Reel

1. Hold the rod with your dominant hand. The reel should be below the rod. The reel foot usually goes between your middle finger and your ring finger, but if it feels better (more balanced) between other fingers, go with that.

2. Pull out or reel in line until you have about six inches of line hanging out of the tip top. Turn the handle slowly until the line roller is directly underneath your index finger.

3. Hold the line against the rod with the crook of your index finger.

4. Open the bail with your other hand.

5. Point the rod at your target.

6. In one smooth motion bring the rod up to vertical.

7. Allow it to flex (the tip bends back behind you, this is called "loading" the rod) without pausing, then start to push the rod forward. Note that the movement is happening in your elbow and wrist, not at the shoulder.

8. When the rod tip is halfway to your target, let go of the line with your index finger to send the lure flying (hopefully at your target). This step is all about timing.

Bait Cast Reel

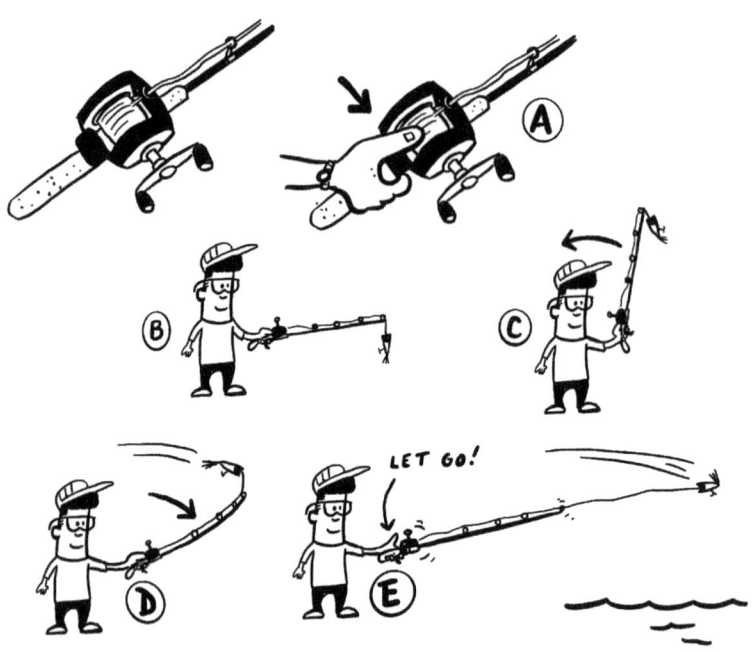

1. Reel in the line. Reel the line in until your bait or lure is 6 to 12 inches (15 to 30 centimeters) from the rod tip. If you have a sinker or bobber attached to the line, it should be 6 to 12 inches from the rod tip instead.

2. Hold the reel properly. Grip the rod behind the reel with your thumb resting over the reel spool. Bait cast rods are designed the same as Spin cast rods. As with Spin cast rods, most fishermen cast with the same hand they retrieve with, so if you prefer to hold the rod behind the reel when you retrieve, you'll need to switch hands when you cast.
    a. You may want to rest your thumb at a slight angle on the spool instead of pressing the very flat of it on the line. This will give you more control over the flow of the line during the cast.

3. Turn the rod so the reel handles point up. As with spin casting gear, this lets you use your wrist when you cast. If you cast with your opposite hand, the handles should point down.

4. Press the reel spool release button. Bait casting reels made since the 1970s have a mechanism to disengage the reel spool from the handles so they don't turn during the cast, allowing for longer casts. The first such models had the button on the side of the reel; most models today feature a release bar behind the spool that you press with your thumb when you rest it on the reel spool.

5. Bend your casting arm. You need to bend your casting arm at the elbow so that the crook of your arm begins to approach a right angle. As you do, raise your rod until its tip goes slightly past vertical. This will give you the correct positioning to send the line out.

6. Sweep the rod forward until it reaches eye level. This is about 30 degrees above horizontal, or the "10 o'clock" position. As you do so, lift your thumb off the reel spool

enough so that the weight of your bait or lure pulls line off the spool as it is propelled toward the target.

    a. If you are casting with a long-handled bait casting rod of the kind used in saltwater fishing, you'll want to use your opposite hand as a fulcrum from which to pivot the rod as you cast.

7. Press down on the reel spool with your thumb to stop the bait when it reaches the target. This is similar to pressing the button on a spin cast reel to brake the line; however, not applying your thumb soon enough leads to the spool continuing to turn after your bait hits the water, creating an overrun or "birds nest" that you'll have to straighten out before you can retrieve your lure.

Spin Cast Reel

(The old faithful)

1. Begin by putting the index finger on the trigger and your thumb on the button of the reel and holding it.//
2. While continuing to hold the button and trigger, bring the fishing rod to one side.
3. With one smooth continuous motion bring the rod forward.
4. When the tip of the fishing rod is even with your body, release the trigger.

5. Re-engage the lock by turning the handle and begin your retrieval.

6. Now reel in your bait and wait for the nibble.

Things to Think About

A - Admit I'm not alone. **A** - Admit I'm a sinner and

B - Believe that God will get me through this. **B** - Believe that Jesus is God's Son and that He died

C - Be Calm and Creative **C** - Confess publicly that Jesus is my Lord and Savior

God says to, "Be still and know I am God" (Psalm 46:1).

Are you stopping and listening to God? Are you reading His Word every day? Are you asking for guidance—not just to get through your situation, but where does He need you the most?

Ponder a moment and then write your path where God is leading you.

_____
_____
_____

8
Foiled Again
What if I don't have my pack?

Scripture
We are in this together.
1 Samuel 30:23-25
David replied, "No, my brothers, you must not do that with what the LORD has given us. He has protected us and delivered into our hands the raiding party that came against us. Who will listen to what you say? The share of the man who stayed with the supplies is to be the same as that of him who went down to the battle. All will share alike." David made this a statute and ordinance for Israel from that day to this.

God supplies all my needs.
1 Chronicles 12:39-40
The men spent three days there with David, eating and drinking, for their families had supplied provisions for them. Also, their neighbors from as far away as Issachar, Zebulun and Naphtali came bringing food on donkeys, camels, mules and oxen. There were plentiful supplies of flour, fig cakes, raisin cakes, wine, olive oil, cattle and sheep, for there was joy in Israel.

When I'm thankful for what I'm given, I'm blessed.
2 Corinthians 9:9-11
As it is written: "They have freely scattered their gifts to the poor; their righteousness endures forever." Now he who supplies seed to the sower and bread for food will also supply and increase your store of seed and will enlarge the harvest of your righteousness. You will be enriched in every way so that you can be generous on every occasion, and through us your generosity will result in thanksgiving to God.

Everything you have around you is a resource.
So many times we get into a situation and forget to take inventory of what we already have. God will supply you with what you need;

you just have to trust Him and let Him show you what you need to do.

STOP, STEP BACK, and LOOK!

What do I have around me that I can use?

Everything has a purpose, including you.

EVERYTHING IS A RESOURCE

Everything has a Purpose, including you.

USE IT!

Aluminum foil -
    Cook with it, boil water, make char cloth, use for signaling
Foil gum wrapper -
    Use for signaling, starting a fire, to wrap a small object in
Old paper -
    Use to start a fire, write a note on, insulation
Old 2-liter bottle -

Make a filter for water, carry water, make a gas mask, make a scoop, fish trap

Plastic cup -
Carry food I find in the woods, carry water, drink from

Old rag or a bandana -
Use as a water filter, use instead of toilet paper, make char cloth, use for gas mask filter

French fry on the floor of the car -
Use to help start a fire or bait for a snare

Soda can -
Use the tab for a hook for fishing, cut the can open and make a signal, make a small stove

Glass soda bottle -
Carry water, a weapon, break the bottom off and use as a magnifying glass for fire

Piece of board -
Use to start a fire, keep a fire going, a weapon, a shelf in my shelter

Bolt laying on the ground -
Use for a weight in fishing, sharpen and make an arrowhead

Potato chip -
Use to start a fire, use to bait a snare trap

Old shoe -
Use the string for cordage, use the sole to replace my shoe, string for a bow

Roll of cable or wire -
Use as cordage or for electrical needs, snare wire for a trap

Drinking straw -

With a rag to filter water, a weapon, piping, sealed container

Egg carton -
Use for fire starter, water filter, carrying tray

Lip balm or crayon -
Use as a candle, use as a sealant

Chip bag or snack wrapper -
Use for signaling, carrying or cooking food

Paper clip - s
mall hook, needle, trigger for a snare

Sock -
water filter, gas mask filter, lint to start fire

Plastic grocery bag -
carry items, capture water, carry water

The best way to be prepared?

Trusting in God. Believe He will provide and He will get you through this.

What do you trust God with?

_____
_____
_____
_____
_____

9
Food – Catching, Finding, Cooking, and Utensils

What can I eat?

Scripture
Job 24:4-6
They thrust the needy from the path and force all the poor of the land into hiding. Like wild donkeys in the desert, the poor go about their labor of foraging food; the wasteland provides food for their children. They gather fodder in the fields and glean in the vineyards of the wicked.

Psalm 111:4-6
He has caused his wonders to be remembered; the LORD is gracious and compassionate. He provides food for those who fear him; he remembers his covenant forever. He has shown his people the power of his works, giving them the lands of other nations.

Acts 14:16-18
In the past, he let all nations go their own way. Yet he has not left himself without testimony: He has shown kindness by giving you rain from heaven and crops in their seasons; he provides you with plenty of food and fills your hearts with joy." Even with these words, they had difficulty keeping the crowd from sacrificing to them.

Edibles in the Wild - What plants can I eat?

Did you know - There are plants you can eat. There are some plants that you can't eat. **Some plants are POISONOUS!**

Some plants can kill you.
When you are in a survival situation, it is important to know what plants are safe, and what plants are dangerous.
Every region has different plants. It is a smart idea to keep a reference manual for your region to help you identify the many types of plants.

Check with your local wildlife agency to find resources that you can keep in your backpack to guide you if you are ever in a survival situation.

Because there are so many types of plants, it is best to learn about the plants in your area. (there are too many to cover in this book!)

Remember - If you are not sure about a plant, **do not eat it**. It could be poisonous or deadly.

      Foraging for plants is good and can fill your hunger, but it will not keep you strong. It is kind of like going to church and worshiping God every now and then. You can get something out of it, but it doesn't continually build your faith.

      Foraging and hunting will make you strong. Protein and plants is like worshiping God with your whole heart. The plants fill you and the protein strengthens you.

      How is your diet with God? Are you still hungry? Are you being fed? Ask God, What more can I do?

_____
_____
_____

Catching or Hunting

You can also catch small game for food. Some small game are birds, mice, squirrels, and rabbits. Depending on your resources will determine what you will be able to catch. Fishing is the best and easiest way to get protein when in a survival situation, but here are a few traps you can set.

REMEMBER ALWAYS, NEVER LEAVE A TRAP SET IF YOU ARE THROUGH WITH IT. You don't want to kill one of God's creatures if you are not there to eat it.

There are different kinds of traps you can set: Dead Fall, Snare, and Cage. Each are used for different purposes.

So how do you know what kind of animals are around? You have to find animal trails and tracks. Trails will be a narrow, worn trail in the woods or grass that has animal tracks on it. Here are some tracks to watch for good and bad.

SPECIAL NOTE

This is not a game or something fun to do— this is survival. We treat God's creatures with respect. ***We only kill to eat.***

SQUIRREL
They dig holes to store nuts they find on the ground. A pole snare is the easiest way to catch them.

RACCOON

They are very smart and a ground snare is your best bet. It may take a couple of times to catch one. Also, they can get up to 40lbs.

BEAVER
You will have to be close to water. It will be easy to find them; just look for the gnawed trees. Be sure to use a strong tree with your ground snare. They can weigh as much as 50 lbs.

RABBIT

They are fast and smart, so make sure that your snare is strong. Look for trails and rabbit burrows in the ground.

WHITE-FOOTED MOUSE
This will be a dead fall trap. You will create a trigger and use a heavy rock or log.

WILD HOG

This is not a good sign. They are very dangerous and run around in small herds. They have tusks that can cut you up. It is best to leave that area and make camp somewhere else or you will have to sleep in a tree.

Snares and Traps

Squirrel Snare

Cage snare

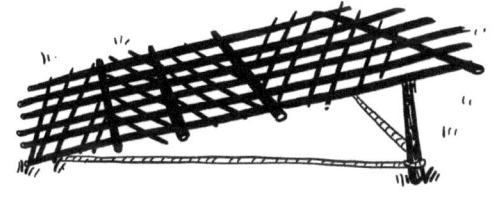

Dead Fall Trap

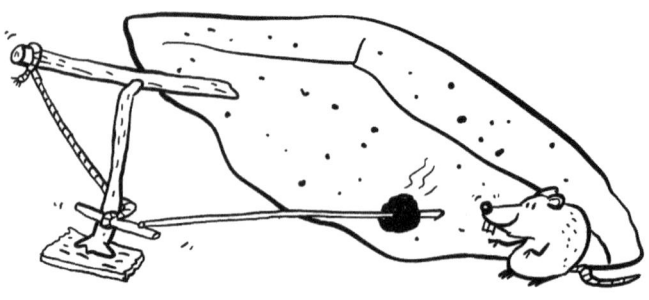

You need 2 sticks that are about as big around as a soda bottle top, a long stick about as big around as your pinky finger, and then a small stick about as big around as your pinky finger (maybe as long as your middle finger). Your bait will depend on what you are trying to catch. If you have peanut butter, berries, seeds, cheese, or chips, all of these will attract a field rat, field mouse, squirrel, or even a bird. You want the rock to be at least bigger than a notebook binder and weigh about 10 to 20 lbs. Give it a day before you go back and check on the trap. It will give your scent a chance to go away.

Field Dressing

Now you have to clean and cook what you have caught.
Just like a fish, the animal must be gutted and cleaned.
DON'T DO THIS NEAR YOUR CAMP!!!
You will attract unwanted visitors.

(like skunks!)

Small rodents, like a field mouse or chipmunk, you can just gut and put on the fire. Let the fire burn off the hairs and eat bones and all because, it is so small.

Life is precious. Blood had to be spilled for forgiveness of sin. Jesus gave His life to save yours. These creatures God gave you are giving their life to save yours. Can you stand up and tell someone what Jesus has done in your life? What would you say?

_____
_____
_____

When cleaning your animal, it is important to clean out the bad—just like Jesus does with your sins when you accept Him as your Savior. Who is Jesus to you? Do you feel bad when you do wrong?

_____
_____
_____

10
Mental Survival
Am I letting God lead me each day?

Scripture
Proverbs 1:2-7 -
We gain wisdom by listening to the Lord.
for gaining wisdom and instruction; for understanding words of insight; for receiving instruction in prudent behavior, doing what is right and just and fair; for giving prudence to those who are simple, knowledge and discretion to the young—let the wise listen and add to their learning, and let the discerning get guidance— for understanding proverbs and parables, the sayings and riddles of the wise. The fear of the LORD is the beginning of knowledge, but fools despise wisdom and instruction.

Exodus 18:18-20 -
We are not alone. God is with us and we need to focus on Him.
"You and these people who come to you will only wear yourselves out. The work is too heavy for you; you cannot handle it alone. Listen now to me and I will give you some advice, and may God be with you. You must be the people's representative before God and bring their disputes to him. Teach them his decrees and instructions, and show them the way they are to live and how they are to behave."

Numbers 12:4-9 - God speaks to us so we should listen.
At once the LORD said to Moses, Aaron and Miriam, "Come out to the tent of meeting, all three of you." So the three of them went out. Then the LORD came down in a pillar of cloud; he stood at the entrance to the tent and summoned Aaron and Miriam. When the two of them stepped forward, he said, "Listen to my words:

"When there is a prophet among you, I, the LORD,
reveal myself to them in visions, I speak to them in dreams.
But this is not true of my servant Moses; he is faithful in all my house. With him I speak face to face, clearly and not in riddles; he sees the form of the LORD. Why then were you not afraid to speak against my servant Moses?"

The anger of the LORD burned against them, and he left them.

Psalm 23 -
The Lord is always with me and He will love and protect me.
The LORD is my shepherd, I lack nothing.
He makes me lie down in green pastures, he leads me beside quiet waters, he refreshes my soul. He guides me along the right paths for his name's sake. Even though I walk through the darkest valley, I will fear no evil, for you are with me; your rod and your staff, they comfort me. You prepare a table before me in the presence of my enemies. You anoint my head with oil; my cup overflows. Surely your goodness and love will follow me all the days of my life, and I will dwell in the house of the LORD forever.

This is why you should keep in your pack a small New Testament or Bible, a note pad, and a pencil. Prayer and reading His Word will help you stay focused on the task at hand: SURVIVAL.

It will not be easy, but KNOW this: God is with you through all of it. You must trust that He will get you through this situation and get you back home. Trust in Him to lead you, but you must do the action and keep going until you make it where you need to be. You can do it because God is with you.

How do you feel about Jesus?
_____
_____
_____

This is why the ABC's of Survival are so important, just like the ABC's of becoming a Christian are important.

A - Admit I'm a sinner,

B - Believe that Jesus is God's Son who was fully human and fully God, and that He died for your sins and rose from the grave, and

C - Confess publicly that you have asked Jesus to be your Lord and Savior and that you want Him to rule over your life.

The ABC's of Survival are similar.

If we know and trust that God will get us through whatever the world throws at us, then I can overcome anything.

"I can do all things through Christ who strengthens me."
Philippians 4:13

If I'm trusting God to handle and take care of things, then I have no worries.

Am I mentally ready? Am I taking the time each day to honor and worship God, my Lord Jesus?

What are things you can do to keep God as your mental focus?

_____
_____
_____
_____
_____
_____

Am I trusting Him in all I do? What am I doing to be closer to Jesus in my heart?

_____
_____
_____
_____
_____
_____

11
Signaling for Help
How will they find me?

Scripture
Genesis 49:24-26 -
He is there to help me in my time of need.
But his bow remained steady, his strong arms stayed limber, because of the hand of the Mighty One of Jacob, because of the Shepherd, the Rock of Israel, because of your father's God, who helps you, because of the Almighty, who blesses you with blessings of the skies above, blessings of the deep springs below, blessings of the breast and womb. Your father's blessings are greater than the blessings of the ancient mountains, than the bounty of the age-old hills. Let all these rest on the head of Joseph, on the brow of the prince among his brothers.

Joshua 24:6-8 -
He hears my cries for help and helps me.
"When I brought your people out of Egypt, you came to the sea, and the Egyptians pursued them with chariots and horsemen as far as the Red Sea. But they cried to the Lord for help, and he put darkness between you and the Egyptians; he brought the sea over them and covered them. You saw with your own eyes what I did to the Egyptians. Then you lived in the wilderness for a long time. I brought you to the land of the Amorites who lived east of the Jordan. They fought against you, but I gave them into your hands. I destroyed them from before you, and you took possession of their land."

Numbers 10:6-8 -
Am I making noise where I can be found?
"At the sounding of a second blast, the camps on the south are to set out. The blast will be the signal for setting out. To gather the assembly, blow the trumpets, but not with the signal for setting out. The sons of Aaron, the priests, are to blow the trumpets. This is to be a lasting ordinance for you and the generations to come.

Zechariah 10:7-9 -
It may take a bit, but my signal will be seen and I will be rescued. "The Ephraimites will become like warriors, and their hearts will be glad as with wine. Their children will see it and be joyful; their hearts will rejoice in the LORD. I will signal for them and gather them in. Surely I will redeem them; they will be as numerous as before. Though I scatter them among the peoples, yet in distant lands they will remember me. They and their children will survive, and they will return."

"I'm Lost!" Now what?

- Am I trying to be found?
- Am I trying to get someone to stop and help me?
- Is there someone after me and I'm trying to signal the right people to help me?
- How can I be found?

There are many different ways to signal for help:
Whistle, Fire, Flags, SOS signs, Mirrors, and Flashlights

- What are my resources?
- What is my situation that I need help?
- In my current location can I be seen or heard to get help?

Remember desperate people do desperate things. Keep your wits about you and always be on the lookout for what you need in your particular situation.

The same thing applies with your spiritual life.

- Am I asking the right questions?
- Are my prayers all about me or am I thanking and loving God?

The Lord's Prayer is an example. Let God know you love Him and that you are thankful for your blessings. To get help you must ask, just like when you ask Jesus for help.

What is it you need to pray for most at this point in your life? (See Matthew 7:7.)

_____
_____
_____

What are my resources?

Whistle - Will I be heard from where I am?
Do I need to get to an elevation or area that I can be heard? The whistle is a high-pitched noise that others will hear from a distance. Don't just do steady blows, mix it up and have a pattern so others know you need help.

Fire - Can they see the light of my fire? I can put green cedar branches on my fire and make white smoke. Am I where they can see that to help me get help? Should I make more than 1 fire to have multiple signals going on, so they can see me better?

Flags - Do I have bright or neon colored cloth that will attract someone's attention? Is it big enough that it can be seen from far away?

SOS signal - Do I have room to make an SOS sign where it can be seen from the air? Can I get logs and spell it out on the ground and light it with fire for people to see me? What materials can I use so that it can be seen?

Mirrors – Can I get where the sun can reflect light to let someone know where I am? I could use a mirror or any shiny reflect surface (e.g., signal mirror, car mirror, aluminum foil, emergency blanket).

Flashlight - I can wave it around so people can see me. Use any kind of light source that you can wave around that is not a normal pattern.

If you're not in a safe place to signal, then you might have to find help on your own. Look for a police officer, fire, ambulance, hospital, police station, a business that you can get an adult to help you.

There are different types of flags that are recognized all over the world that tell people what your needs are:
A white flag means truce or surrender or help.

A red flag with a white cross or white flag with a red cross means either you need medical attention or you are giving medical attention.

An orange flag means caution or be aware.

A red flag means stop or danger.

Making an S.O.S. or Signal of Stress Sign

It can be on the vehicle you are in, the top of your tent or tarp, it can even be drawn out on the ground. Where are you located that people will see it and send help?

The SOS is Morse code (... --- ...) that means I need help. Also, the letter X is another symbol that is well known for rescue. If you are where a small plane or helicopter can fly over and see your sign to be rescued, then you want to use this.

Also, if there are rescue planes or helicopters flying over looking for you and your family, a signal mirror is also a great way to let them know where you are. Hold your hand in front of you and let the sun reflect on to your hand, open your hand with like a V or peace sign and then aim the reflection at the overhead plane or helicopter, now wiggle the mirror back and forth so they will see where you are.

Signaling is also what we do as Christians. We show others that we are a follower of Christ by our actions in public. Are you giving off the right signals?

How are you showing others you are a Christian?

_____
_____
_____
_____
_____
_____

12
Sleep & Rest – Staying Warm & Dry
Am I re-energizing or not?

Scripture
Genesis 2:1-3 -
God said we need to rest and gave us an example.
Thus the heavens and the earth were completed in all their vast array. By the seventh day God had finished the work he had been doing; so on the seventh day he rested from all his work. Then God blessed the seventh day and made it holy, because on it he rested from all the work of creating that he had done.

Genesis 18:3-5 -
Rest, eat and be refreshed. You have to take time and rest or you want make it. He said, "If I have found favor in your eyes, my lord, do not pass your servant by. Let a little water be brought, and then you may all wash your feet and rest under this tree. Let me get you something to eat so, you can be refreshed and then go on your way—now that you have come to your servant."
"Very well," they answered, "do as you say."

1 Chronicles 22:17-19 -
I need to rest so I can focus on the path that God wants me to follow. Then David ordered all the leaders of Israel to help his son Solomon. He said to them, "Is not the LORD your God with you? And has he not granted you rest on every side? For he has given the inhabitants of the land into my hands, and the land is subject to the LORD and to his people. Now devote your heart and soul to seeking the LORD your God. Begin to build the sanctuary of the LORD God, so that you may bring the ark of the covenant of the LORD and the sacred articles belonging to God into the temple that will be built for the Name of the LORD."

Psalm 16:8-10 -
He watches over me as I rest so, I can be refreshed.
I keep my eyes always on the LORD. With him at my right hand, I will not be shaken. Therefore my heart is glad and my tongue

rejoices; my body also will rest secure, because you will not abandon me to the realm of the dead, nor will you let your faithful one see decay.

Matthew 11:27-29 -
Christ promises peace and rest in Him.
"All things have been committed to me by my Father. No one knows the Son except the Father, and no one knows the Father except the Son and those to whom the Son chooses to reveal him. "Come to me, all you who are weary and burdened, and I will give you rest. Take my yoke upon you and learn from me, for I am gentle and humble in heart, and you will find rest for your souls."

If you don't rest, you will not last 2 days in the wilderness. When you are under stress from a situation, stop a moment and just breathe and rest. Build your shelter, make your fire, filter your water, and get a bite to eat, then just sit down and rest. Read your Bible, make notes about the day in your note pad, make a list of what you need to do so that you are not stressing on what your next step is. The more you can take off your mind and give to God to take care of, the better rest you will get.

When I don't get enough sleep, I get what is called sleep deprivation. This can cause your body to do some strange things and play tricks on your mind.

Symptoms of Sleep Deprivation
- Hallucinations
- Confusion
- Loss of memory
- Hand tremors
- Headaches
- Increases in blood pressure
- Elevated stress hormone levels
- Extreme irritability

This is why you need to rest. Also, stay hydrated! Make your shelter feel as safe as you need it to be so you can rest. Even though it is only for 1 or 2 nights, make it comfortable. This is why you need to be PREPARED for whatever comes.

You don't know what the situation may be where you need to survive. It could be an accident and you are the only survivor. It could be a natural disaster like a tornado, flood, hurricane, or even an earthquake.

ARE YOU PREPARED?

God is there for you: "For God so loved the world that he gave his one and only Son, that whoever believes in him shall not perish but have eternal life. For God did not send his Son into the world to condemn the world, but to save the world through him" (John 3:16-17).

Sleep helps you in these 5 ways:
1. Restores the body
2. Reduces stress
3. Reduces illness
4. Improves memory
5. Improves physical reflexes

Try to get 7 to 9 hours sleep if you can. If you don't get a lot at night, take a few 10-minute naps as the day goes on, this will help refresh you for a little while.

We need rest and to spend time with God.
When you stop, don't speak, don't think—just listen. Hear all that God has created. It is all there for you. Are you taking time each day to stop, look, and listen? Are you making quiet time to be with the Lord? What do you do to have peace with the Lord each day?

13

First Aid

Am I clean?

Scripture
Isaiah 58:8-10 –
You must stay calm and focus on the healing and prayerfully do the task. "Then your light will break forth like the dawn, and your healing will quickly appear; then your righteousness will go before you, and the glory of the Lord will be your rear guard. Then you will call, and the Lord will answer; you will cry for help, and he will say: Here am I. If you do away with the yoke of oppression, with the pointing finger and malicious talk, and if you spend yourselves in behalf of the hungry and satisfy the needs of the oppressed, then your light will rise in the darkness, and your night will become like the noonday."

Ezekiel 47:11-12 -
All injuries are not the same, I can't save everyone. I can only do my best, trust God. "But the swamps and marshes will not become fresh; they will be left for salt. Fruit trees of all kinds will grow on both banks of the river. Their leaves will not wither, nor will their fruit fail. Every month they will bear fruit, because the water from the sanctuary flows to them. Their fruit will serve for food and their leaves for healing."

Psalm 106:3-5 –
I should be thankful and praise God for His healing and guiding my hand. Blessed are those who act justly, who always do what is right. Remember me, Lord, when you show favor to your people, come to my aid when you save them, that I may enjoy the prosperity of your chosen ones, that I may share in the joy of your nation and join your inheritance in giving praise.

What do I need to have in my first aid kit?

What is important?

Can I prepare for every situation?

The first thing you need is a watertight container to carry your first aid in, otherwise it will not be clean and sterile. Medical supplies need to stay dry and sterile so germs won't spread. The list below is recommended.

My First Aid Kit

4–6	Band-Aids	for small cuts
2	2" Gauze	for larger wounds that need packing
1	4" Gauze	packing large wounds
2–3	Alcohol	helps kill the germs on the wound
2–3	Antibiotic	helps the wound heal
1	Small	to cut bandages or bandage tape
1 roll	Bandage	to tape down wounds
2–3	Aspirin or	helps with pain
1	Sewing	to sew up a wound
2 or 3	Benadryl	for allergic reactions
1	Super Glue/ Liquid stitch	to seal up wounds without sewing
1	Tweezers	for getting out splinters and other
1 pair	Latex gloves	for sterile use

Your Bible is like your Spiritual First Aid.

Reading it is healing and inspirational. Are you getting your daily healing? What is your favorite scripture?

_____
_____
_____

CPR

It would be good to learn this not just for survival but for everyday life too.

How to Clean a Wound in the Wilderness

Anytime you are in the wilderness you have the potential to be wounded. Always keep a clean bandage on a wound or it will get infected.

While most wounds are not serious and do not require much more than cleaning, others can be serious. If a wound is dirty, deep, or tissue is damaged, it is important to clean it well. Having a first aid kit with the necessary tools will make your job much easier.

An irrigation syringe is an important tool for wounds. It can be used to run clean water over a wound after you wash it with soap. This helps remove debris and infection causing substances.

- ➢ Having some cotton swabs on hand can help you apply any antibiotic ointment needed after flushing the wound.
- ➢ Gauze is also a good thing to have, so you can cover the wound once it is clean.
- ➢ Ointments such as triple antibiotic or Neosporin are best for wounds.
- ➢ Cloth medical tape can be used to hold the gauze in place once you are finished with the dressing.
- ➢ While wound care in the wild is not ideal, it is an important step to avoiding infections.

Treating a Sprain or Twisted Ankle

If you are active in the wilderness, you may end up with sprains at some point. This is an injury that plagues hikers and rock climbers but can affect anyone. Sprains are ligament injuries that occur when the fibers are partially torn. This causes pain, swelling, and difficulty in movement. Knees, ankles, and elbows are the most commonly sprained joints.

Minor sprains are often soothed using the RICE method, which stands for:

- Rest
- Ice
- Compression
- Elevate

Apply cold packs for the first 24 hours after injury. After that, heat packs may reduce the pain best. You should have compression bandages in your first aid kit and OTC pain medications to ease the discomfort. Knowing how to treat sprains before you are in the field is key to getting the pain under control fast.

Learn the Heimlich Maneuver

Recognize Dehydration Early

Dehydration can happen very fast when you are outdoors in the sun and heat, particularly when you are active. This condition can be sneaky and symptoms can occur suddenly. Dehydration happens when you lose more body fluids than you take in. When you are busy outdoors, it can be easy to forget to drink enough water or sports drinks. This means your body is in need of fluid, especially after urinating and sweating. Dehydration can happen to anyone, but babies and elderly people are at the greatest risk.

If you have babies or small children, it is always best to be sure they have adequate fluid intake while you are outside. The best way to treat dehydration is to prevent it from happening in the first place. Dehydration can be serious. If you see the early warning signs of dehydration, you must get medical attention quickly to avoid serious complications. Get them to drink water and rest ASAP!!!

Treating Burns Correctly
Burns are one of the most painful injuries you can have. Unfortunately, burns occur often while camping in the wilderness.

> **Lighting campfires and cooking over an open flame are two ways many people get burned outdoors.**

If this happens to you, it is important to know how to treat burns correctly.

You will need to know the difference in treating chemical burns and burns from heat sources like fire. In addition, everyone in your party needs to know how to stop, drop and roll to prevent fire from spreading.

Quick action is key to reducing the amount of area burned on the body. Mild burns are more easily treated in the wilderness than severe burns. However, if anyone suffers a serious and painful burn, medical treatment must be sought.

Bone and Joint Injuries
A dislocated shoulder or a broken arm needs a sling with a triangle bandage

OR

Sprained Ankle

Bad Cut—What to Do

Special note: Cayenne pepper is great for clotting a wound, but don't get it on your hands or in your eye. You can put it in a serious wound and it will stop the bleeding.

If the cut is a deep cut and you don't think you can sew it up, you can use Super Glue.

Clean the wound really well and try and stop the bleeding. Then pull the wound together and apply the Super Glue. Let it dry and then get a couple of small strips of duct tape and pull the wound together. This is a temporary fix but will hold for a couple of days. The injured person needs to rest and not move around a lot so the wound can heal.

How to Remove a Tick

Be sure to spray yourself with bug repellant to help keep unwanted bugs off of you. Smoke is another odor that will keep bugs away from you. Also, the oils from cedar tree branches can be crushed and rubbed on to keep bugs away.

Your first aid kit will have more information for treating different kinds of wounds.

This is another reason to get a GOOD first aid kit to put in your bag. It may save your life.

Spiritual wounds can be just as bad as physical wounds. Have faith that God will get you through this. Think about all He has already helped you overcome.

List your blessings:

_____
_____
_____

14
Archery (Protection & Hunting)
How can I provide food for my family and protect them?

Scripture
Deuteronomy 23:14 -
Desperate times means there will be desperate people, PROTECT YOURSELF!For the LORD your God moves about in your camp to protect you and to deliver your enemies to you. Your camp must be holy, so that he will not see among you anything indecent and turn away from you.

Psalm 5:10-12 -
Keep your guard up, God is with you but, be on your guard. Declare them guilty, O God! Let their intrigues be their downfall. Banish them for their many sins, for they have rebelled against you. But let all who take refuge in you be glad; let them ever sing for joy. Spread your protection over them; that those who love your name may rejoice in you. Surely, LORD, you bless the righteous; you surround them with your favor as with a shield.

Genesis 27:2-4 -
You have to eat, if there is no place to fish, you need protein. Isaac said, "I am now an old man and don't know the day of my death. Now then, get your equipment—your quiver and bow—and go out to the open country to hunt some wild game for me. Prepare me the kind of tasty food I like and bring it to me to eat, so that I may give you my blessing before I die."

Proverbs 12:26-28 -
The food will not come to you—you must be stealthy and only take what you NEED. The righteous choose their friends carefully, but the way of the wicked leads them astray. The lazy do not roast any game, but the diligent feed on the riches of the hunt. In the way of righteousness there is life; along that path is immortality.

Why Archery?

Why not have a gun? Well, with archery, you can make a bow in a couple of hours and you're ready to go. With a gun, you have to have bullets. Once you have shot those bullets, the gun is useless. With a bow, you can make new arrows or retrieve the arrows you shot. You can make different kinds of arrows to hunt different game or protect yourself. Also, archery is quiet and stealthy. If you miss your target, you have a chance to shoot again; a gun makes noise and scares the prey away.

BE SAFE
Never touch a gun without **adult supervision**.
Never use a bow and arrow (archery) without adult supervision.
These are very dangerous, lethal, and are not toys.

There are many different kinds of bows. There are Long Bows, Recurve Bows, Compound Bows, and Crossbows.

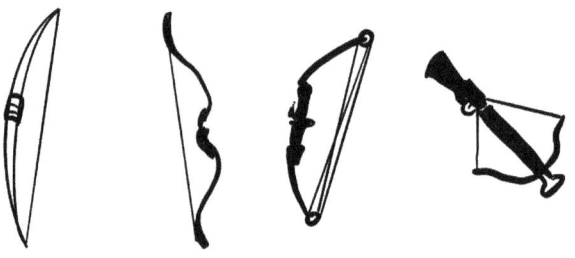

*** These are TOOLS not TOYS ***

How do I need to stand when firing a bow?

A good shooting stance should be relaxed with good posture. Don't slouch. Your feet should be straddling your imaginary shooting line a shoulders width apart. Your toes should be pointing straight in front of you. Then your left side of your body should be

lined up with your target, if you are right handed. Then point your left foot at an angle, just slightly, so you can keep your balance. The top of your right foot should have an imaginary line going straight to the bulls-eye on the target. Turn your head to the left and see your target, where you are aiming for, and lift the bow with your left hand and your right hand pull back the string at the same time. Breathe in your nose at the same time and release the breath right before you fire. If your left handed everything will be the opposite.

How do I hold my bow?

Set First holding a bow is not like shaking a hand, you do not try and squeeze it really hard. You want to grip the bow handle with the meaty part of your hand, just below your thumb. You are mainly gripping with your thumb and your first two fingers. Your hand will be at an angle so that you pinky finger doesn't touch the handle at all. Hold it relaxed, remember you're not shaking a hand.

How do I hold the string and how do I shoot the bow?

You want to use three fingers. Your index finger goes above the nock and the other two go below. You only want to hold the string at your first joint to the middle of your fingerprint. The pinky finger doesn't touch the string. You will pull back the string, keeping your elbow level with your shoulder. The string should be pulled back so the string touches your cheek on the side you are pulling back with. Now you should be able to look straight down the arrow and see the target. Remember to breathe and fire.

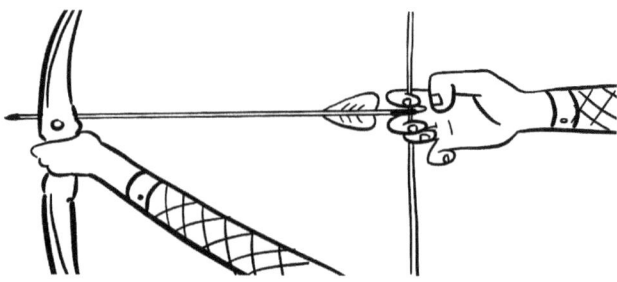

NEVER FIRE IF SOMEONE IS OUT IN FRONT OF YOU. Safety first. (Some people like to rest their thumb at the crease of their mouth on their cheek when drawing the string back to fire)
You will feel the muscles in your shoulder and your back get tired the more you fire the bow. These are the muscles that you need to strengthen when using a bow.

If using a sight, that means you are shooting at a distance, remember that gravity plays a big part of the arrow hitting its mark. Use your sight to line up your target. You may have to adjust the sight a few times to set it just right. Start with a short distance and then work on a longer distance, with your site. Be sure to shoot each time with the same posture so that the bow will be accurate with the site. Remember when you are at full draw to keep your bow hand where your wrist is at a slight angle. This will keep the bow string from hitting your arm and keep you from having to wear a wrist guard. Take your time on eyeing your target. Patience is important when using your bow and the more you practice the better you will get at hitting the target. Even in a survival situation you should practice shooting. You don't want to wound an animal and not be able to find it. Do not move until you see or hear the arrow hit the target for best accuracy.

Archery Safety

If you are practicing or shooting at a range, always remember, this is a weapon, NOT A TOY.
Never keep an arrow in the bow, unless you are about to fire the bow.
Never point the bow at anything but your target, when loaded.

God says that we are to lean on His understanding and acknowledge Him in all we do and He will direct our paths (Proverbs 3:5-6). Just like your bow, you need to keep you shot straight. You cannot rush it.

Are you letting God lead you or are you doing whatever you want?

What are you doing to stay on the path?

Just like in archery, our faith needs to be straight and strong. Sometimes it is hard to stay on target because of the distractions of the world, but stop, breathe, and focus.

List the things that distract you from God:

_____
_____
_____
_____
_____

Now you know what to overcome, and knowing is half the battle.

15
Tools
Do I have tools or do I need to make them?

Scripture
Genesis 4:21-22 - I can create the tools I need because God supplies the materials. His brother's name was Jubal; he was the father of all who play stringed instruments and pipes. Zillah also had a son, Tubal-Cain, who forged all kinds of tools out of bronze and iron. Tubal-Cain's sister was Naamah.

Exodus 31:3-5 - God gives me my skills and knowledge on what to do. "And I have filled him with the Spirit of God, with wisdom, with understanding, with knowledge and with all kinds of skills—to make artistic designs for work in gold, silver and bronze, to cut and set stones, to work in wood, and to engage in all kinds of crafts."

Isaiah 44:12 - Use the tools and knowledge the right way, for God. The blacksmith takes a tool and works with it in the coals; he shapes an idol with hammers, he forges it with the might of his arm. He gets hungry and loses his strength; he drinks no water and grows faint.

The tools in my bag:

The tools I have in my bag is one less thing I have to make to survive. Yes, I can make a cutting tool by getting a rock and breaking off the edges and rubbing it against a flat rock to put an edge on it, but after all of the effort put out to make that one tool, I will have burned through all my calories.

I can make my own rope or cordage using grass or vines, but it is better to have it in my bag ready to go.

My tools help me to survive.

Everything that I should have in my bag should have more than one use for it.

Just as an example:

Duct tape can be used to seal a wound, make a repair on my tent, tarp, or poncho, make a pair of shoes, make rope or cordage, and even a bag to carry things with.

Everything that you have is a resource. From the shirt you are wearing to the shoelaces on your feet. Think outside the box when you are in a survival situation. You never know what you may need and for what you may need it for.

**What kinds of tools should I keep in my bag?
Here are a lot of tools you have seen over the last few weeks:**

- Duct Tape
- Knife
- Compass
- Cordage
- Poncho
- Pencil Sharpener
- Note Pad
- Dental Floss
- Whistle
- Mirror
- Laundry Bag
- Flashlight
- Bandana/Rag
- Flint/Firestarter
- Plastic Bags
- Bible

Keep your bag ready to go at all times.
You should be prepared!!

You have prepared your mind for survival now. God's Word says "Do Not Be Afraid" 365 times, once for every day of the year. There is much more to learn, but more importantly, have you prepared your heart for Jesus?

Who is Jesus to you?
_____
_____
_____

Do you know Him? Would you like to?
_____

Emergency Bag Checklist

- ☐ Bible
- ☐ Notepad & pencil
- ☐ First aid kit (with needle and Super Glue added)
- ☐ First Aid Reference and Instruction Manual
- ☐ Regional Plant Identification Reference Manual
- ☐ Multi-tool
- ☐ Survival knife - Only with adult supervision and permission
- ☐ Water filtration system
- ☐ 550 Paracord (Cordage)
- ☐ Tent or tarp
- ☐ Sleeping bag or blanket
- ☐ Sling/bandana
- ☐ Duct tape
- ☐ Space blanket
- ☐ Water-carrying solution/canteen
- ☐ Food or energy bars that have longer than a year to 3-year shelf life
- ☐ A couple of freeze-dried meals; shelf life is 10 years
- ☐ Change of clothes
- ☐ Matches/fire starter/lighter -Only with adult supervision and permission
- ☐ Glow sticks
- ☐ Flashlights
- ☐ Compass
- ☐ Whistle
- ☐ Dental floss
- ☐ Poncho
- ☐ Pencil sharpener
- ☐ Laundry bag/mosquito netting
- ☐ Small mirror
- ☐ Backpack for your gear

Places where you can get the materials for your bag:
- Local Retailers
- Sporting Goods Stores
- Grocery Stores

Be thrifty but don't be cheap;
it is your survival we are talking about!

Important Knots to Learn

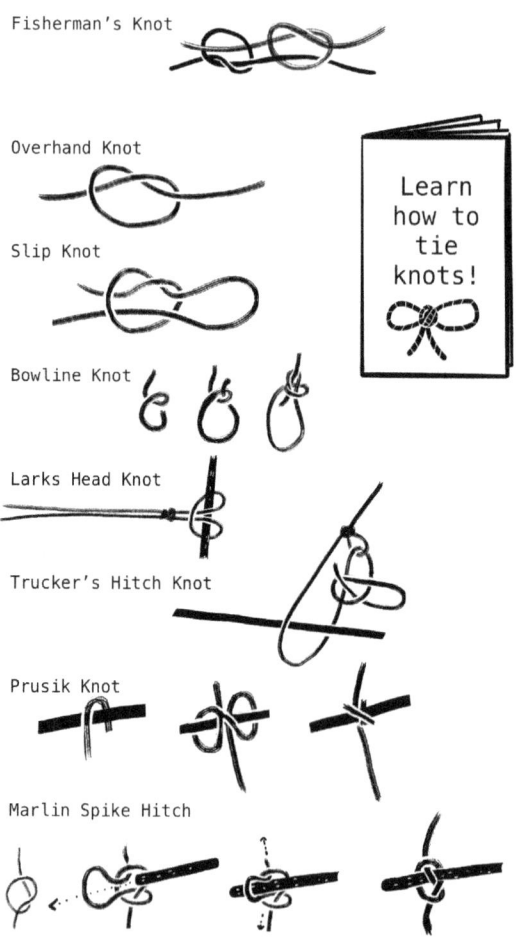

Fisherman's Knot

Overhand Knot

Slip Knot

Bowline Knot

Larks Head Knot

Trucker's Hitch Knot

Prusik Knot

Marlin Spike Hitch

Map to Truth

Last but not least.
Here is your Map to Truth in surviving life:

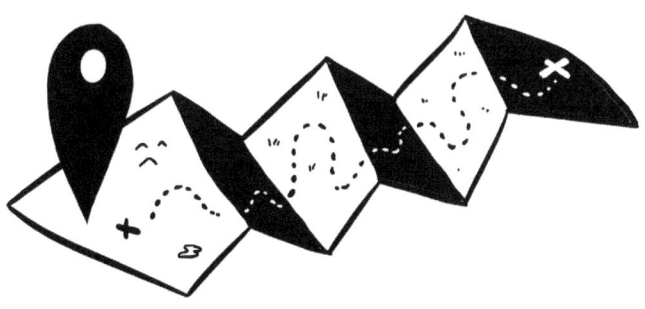

What do I do to become a Christian?

A - Admit I'm a sinner - Romans 3:23 - "for all have sinned and fall short of the glory of God."

B - Believe that Jesus is the Son of God, that He was born and died and rose again to be your Lord and Savior - Romans 5:8 - "But God demonstrates his own love for us in this:
While we were still sinners, Christ died for us."
Romans 6:23 - "For the wages of sin is death, but the gift of God is eternal life in Christ Jesus our Lord."
Romans 10:9 - "If you declare with your mouth, "Jesus is Lord," and believe in your heart that God raised him from the dead, you will be saved."

Your prayer to Jesus asking Him into your life and to be in control of your life:

C - Confess that I have accepted Jesus as my Lord and Savior and that I have asked Him to forgive me of all of my sins.
Romans 10:13 - "Everyone who calls on the name of the Lord will be saved."

There are things you need to do once you have been saved:

1. If you don't have a church home, find one.
2. Get baptized in the Name of the Father, Son, and Holy Spirit
3. Celebrate the Lord's Supper
4. Continue learning about God's Word and the Lord Jesus
5. Fellowship with other Christians
6. Keep a godly heart by reading His Word daily
7. Pray daily

Apply what you have learned.
Seek Him daily to know your path and listen intently to hear The Way.

Congratulations!!!
You have learned the basics of survival in a bad situation and how to make Jesus your Lord and Savior for eternal life.

May God bless you on your journey.

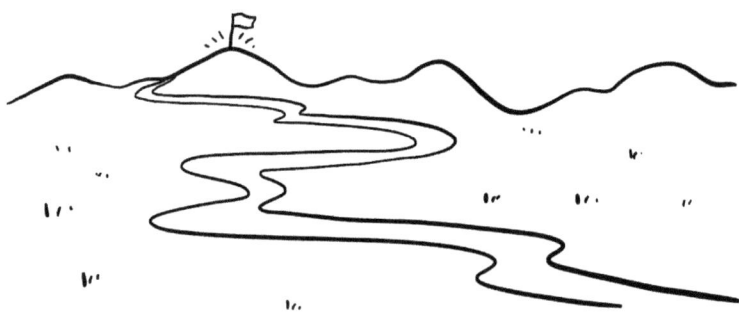